BOUNDARY COMMISSIONS

Kala writes, teaches and lives in Bangalore, with Totoro, Sathyavak, Gauri and Paru. She writes poetry and prose, often losing track of the boundaries between the two. She is enthralled by the workings of language—a chimera she has been chasing much of her working life. She values family, friendship, and her students.

KALA KRISHNAN

BOUNDARY COMMISSIONS

LOVE POEMS

WESTLAND
POETRY

WESTLAND
POETRY

Published by Westland Books, a division of Nasadiya Technologies Private Limited, in 2026

No. 269/2B, First Floor, 'Irai Arul', Vimalraj Street, Nethaji Nagar, Alapakkam Main Road, Maduravoyal, Chennai 600095

ISBN: 9789371970457

10 9 8 7 6 5 4 3 2 1

Typeset by Jojy Philip

Printed at Parksons Graphics Pvt. Ltd

for all the children
—Abhimanyu, Vir, Sathyavak, Shyama, Gauri & Paru—
another compass, for travel across love's shifting continents

CONTENTS

I

Data Collection

WHAT SHE WROTE WHEN HE ASKED HOW HE FIGURES IN HER DEVOTION TO THE GOD OF HILLS AND CAVES

One

she

when he sings
Dhrupad,
she knows that her
words will never fully
be able to say
how she loves him.

he

when she says
she loves him,
he recognises
the same
language
he has heard
in the many
songs he sings.

He

they say, He
is God of both
love and
language;
that's why
He feels cramped
now: for she, and
he—poet and
songster—
make no difference
between the two,
and suddenly he's
one house less.

Two

he

he is a hill
of newly-opened purple
he is a bird
emerald-and-gold-winged
he is not mine
and I am not his, but
the knot is looped and tied,
not thrice, but seven times over.

He

He is the
newly opened
purple kurinji in the hills,
He is the emerald and gold
in bird wings;
He is not mine
and I know this, but
though no knot loops or ties,
in every lifetime, I am His.

Three

He

what,
asks the God,
he comes first now?
and walks
out of her heart

he

the poet's God
and she
can go to their hills
and caves,
he says,
—they can pinch
each other and see
if they're real—
and leaves.

she

her heart lurches,
what? it asks,
what?
neither He, nor he
understands our language.

they

he, she, He: who knows
what's what, but all
three stop
for song.

Four

He

He is God,
there's little doubt
about that
but when he—the
one she's fallen in love
with—sings, it seems the
god has a little trouble
remembering that it is He
who makes
the worlds go round,
His face their sun,
His voice their clarion.

she

she loves them
both—that we know;
what we have
trouble figuring out
is this: when he sings,
who makes her
think of Him—the other
one, the god?
And when the god

storms into her poem,
how is it the other's face
that loops her heart's
hold and pulls it
plummeting
into the well of his song?

he

in all this,
he doesn't want to know
what's happening, but when
she speaks about his song,
he feels like he's on a high hill,
and the music swarms in his throat,
as if the God of Hills had willed it.

Five

She said: I love you.
He said: What!
She said: What I just said.
He said: This is not right.

Is that what you want,
she asked: to be right?
And moved around,
so she was to his left, and
he, on the right.
He threw up his hands,
stamped his foot
and said: I'm going.
She shifted, so her
weight was on
right and left, both,
and said: I will wait.

Her God—the one who
lived on
the high hill—the one with
two wives—smiled. He looked to
his right—His wife was there;
He turned to his
left—one wife was there too.
He looked down

at his poet shifting from
leg to leg.
He left his wives and went
to stand in front of her.
He said: Alone?
She said: You too?
He shifted suddenly, so he
was on her right; she too
shifted, so she stood in front
of him. She said: Lord,
this is right.
He smiled and said: Okay.

The
other one, the songster
who had left when
she said she loved him,
turned around right
then and saw her hold out
her poem to no one:
on her left, there was no one
and on her right, there was
no one.
She and her God smiled at how
wrong he was, and left him
to himself.

Six

Again, she said,
I love you
and again he asked,
'Still? What is this?'
He did that stamping
of the feet and
throwing up
of the hands.
She stood her ground.
And on that high hill,
He smiled, this God of Love.
'Wasn't that
the third?' he asked.
She said,
'Lord, are you counting?
What about earning my
devotion by doing
something helpful?'

Seven

I love you,
she said again to he
she had fallen in love with.
And again, he said, 'What! Still?
This is not right.'
By then, he had become accustomed
to the strange things the words made
her say, so he added, 'It is not left,
either.'
And then, the words took things into
their hands, and unable to stop, he went
on
and on: 'Not left, not left over from an
other birth or left here by anyone,
and there is nothing left
to make of it.'
'Right,' she said, 'you are right.'
And she left him there, standing at the
door of the hall where he was to sing to
people who came to hear songs to
the hill-loving, peacock-riding king
of love and poetry and—let's
not forget—song.

On the high hill, He sat—one to his left,
smiling, and to his right, the second one,

smiling too. They two
had talked of how if there was one
more, that would make a left, a right
and a middle wife.
They shook their heads. One said,
'That can't be right.' The other
added, 'And it won't be left,
either.' They giggled.
He knew there would not be
any other; he wasn't at all taken up
with their clever puns: he had heard
far better, and at the moment, he
was looking at his poet, left
at the door by the one she loved.
He got off his throne and went
to hold her hand.
He said, 'Let's go right now and spend
what's left of this evening watching
clouds from that high hill, there;
that's mine, too.'
She said,
'Lord, that's not right. It's not left
to you or me to decide;
my heart says right now, I must be left
to do what I came to do: listen to him sing.'
'Right,' he said, 'right.'
Then, with a giggle, 'Would that be left,
to me? If it's your right, it must be my left.'
She said, 'My Lord, it is right. When it's
you, it's always right.'

WHAT SHE SAYS WHEN SHE'S TEACHING SANGAM POETS AND HE ASKS HER TO WRITE LIKE THEM, HOW SHE LOVES HIM

One

When I speak
to you,
my chest is
the bank of some
well-travelled river,
where they come
to sing, the poets,
those ones
who, we learn, dealt
with love and verse
as if they were
weighing life
and death.

Two

Your voice
wakes the
bird in its cage
inside my ribs
and without
hesitation,
it spouts a verse
about rain
on
hills
waiting to
sprout.

Three

Your absence, to me,
beloved,
is like that king's question to
the wise ones.
He turned love-play, and love
and romance, into a riddle
that had to be
unlocked by a turn
of words.
He asked about one thing,
but was in fact asking
about something
else.

He asked, that king,
of a bee, flying thither
hither, can you say,
if women's hair
—his face still bearing the
artful fragrances
of the queen's black-as-bees
tresses—
had a natural intoxicating
smell.
And since bee language

was beyond him,
he repeated this doubt,
artificed into verse,
to the wise ones.

To me, this verse asks
the only question
that lovers
—no matter whether they
talk of this or that,
or of nothing—
ever ask: Are you really mine?
Can you really be mine?

Four

Those noble ones, they knew
how the absence of one
of two lovers
could change everything
to nothing.
So they said,
when she cannot come to
meet him:
no stars, no moon, no sun
or rain-clouds in the sky.

No sky.

Five

She dreamed of the
meeting with him—
even the colours on the
forest trees under which
he would wait.

But it was not to be—
she could not leave home.

They tell us the wind was
strong that night;
and the next morning,
the lily-pond in her garden
covered in hill-tree leaves.

Six

She didn't
know
how
to tell him
how much
she loved
him,
so she sent
her household
parrot,
who went, perched
on his shoulder
and
spouted a verse:

they say the clouds
gathered
and
broke and
swarms of
peacocks came
and danced.

Even he can't have
missed the point.

Seven

Even though the
tattoo is on the inside
of her wrist
and cannot be seen
unless she turns
her hand over, she
keeps it hidden when
she's with others,
for
she knows that her eyes
cannot resist winging
to the nectar of his name.

Eight

It seems like
yesterday her friends
were saying that
after she met him,
when he brought
mountain honey to
market,
she's been spending all
her time watching how
the tahr climb.
And now,
she doesn't even
need a handhold
clambering to where
the tree branches hang
heavy with honeycombs.

Nine

She repeatedly told him
she loved him
but he was being proper
and resistant to her wooing.
Now, suddenly, he wants
to know if she really loves
him.
But she's become stubborn,
she tosses her head
and stamps her foot and
says, 'Go ask Pari's hills
if they loved him'.

Later, he remembers
that the wise ones told of
how the trees on Pari's hill
shed all their leaves and stood
bare
when he was taken in battle.
And he smiles.

Ten

They—those noble
ones—
knew that the
alphabets have
life.
They wrote:

her face burns,
her hands
shake, her lips
quiver, her steps
slow, and it seems
her breath will stop,
when the little ones
—learning their
lessons—
come to the
last few of
the alphabets,

and her mother
knows the sound
his name
begins with.

WHAT THE POET SAYS WHEN THE MUSICIAN ASKS HER IF SHE CAN WRITE HIM POEMS FROM RANDOM WORDS IN HER MONIER WILLIAMS

eka: one

ekasaakshika/single-witnessed

No
one was pre-
sent
when the poet lost her
heart;
but every
where she went, every
thing knew: trees
sent their leaves to
fall on her, with
his voice as the BGM,
sleep sent dreams
in which he was hero-ing;
it seems, sometimes
she heard dialogue,
as if someone were
coaching someone else.
It is clear: the invasion

of her heart was
an inside job—
someone who
lived there already
opened
the door to an
other one.
That first One
is the only
One
who witnessed
this: Guha,
Dweller in the
Heartscave.

ekatara/single-stringed

You
are there, Lord.
It seems you
haven't even
noticed what's
going on.
But how,
when he sings,
do I feel plucked?
What fingers
hold, stretch, let go,
so I re-sound?
Maybe the wise ones
were not accurate: you
set poets to music, not poems.

two: dvi

dvi-deha/with two bodies

This is my body:
it burns
like giant stars do
and stills
and melts and
breaks open.

That is my lover's
body:
it skies my
starburns; it up-holds
my stilling, it
gathers my
breakings.
When I melt, it
melts like it were mine.

dvija/twice-born

He enters
inside
me;
everything enters
with him and
we all
take
another birth.

dvi-hridaya/double-hearted (pregnant)

Her heart
had always
danced to the
sound of words.
Now, with his
singing,
her chest feels
the surge of
duets.

three: tri

tribhaga/ the third part, of the eye sending a particular side-glance

The two fish
in his eyes
thrash about
as he passes
her,
then leap
into the
pond of her
heart,
      splashing
them both.

triratrina/ a woman three days after her courses

His friends
had laughed
at his polite
habit of staying
away three in
every twenty-eight
days; now,
he smiles at
how he had thought
anything could
come between
him and her,
least of all, a little blood.

four: uda

uda tantu/water-thread

Embracing,
his sweat
drops
all over
her neck:
married
with a thread
of water.

udanyu/seeking water

Even
a bath in the river
doesn't stop
her from waiting
to be bathed
in his sweat.

WHAT THE POET WROTE, WHEN THE MUSICIAN ASKED FOR POEMS LIKE MUSICAL PHRASES, WITH 'SEA' AND 'HILL'

Sea

i

The
sea was
rowdy
that evening
and every
now and then,
wheeling
seabirds
dived—nose
first, wings folded
—into the foaming
waves.
In the time we
stood there, the
sky darkened, the
wind got heavy:
it was clear
there would be rain.

ii

The waves
were high
and broke so hard,
they sent the wind
careening.
When people
passed by,
your eyes went
to what your
song-stained
lips did on my
neck
at dawn on the
morning after
our first night
there.

iii

That night
the wind was
playful—flinging
sea-wet at the
windows, with
a sandy rustle.
The nesting
gulls were restless
too; the sky was
full of black clouds,
and when they shifted,
the white moon shone
on you, as you bided
your time inside me.

Hill

i

Up there,
on that
very high hill
they call by the name
of their myth-housed
ancestor, I realised
just how close
the hill's rim was,
only when I stumbled
and you grabbed
my shoulder
so tight, it stung.

ii

The indigo
of my mukkuti
must have
turned black
then,
when you
clasped my face
to you, and
your eyes ran over,
there on that

high hill of their
ancestors, its rim
camouflaged by
wandering clouds.

iii
Then
you picked me
up,
your tears on
my face still,
and behind the
fiery boulder, did
with me what men do
with women they love;
the hill loomed all
around us,
with the bones of
generations of our
friend's ancestors, he
having told us, in his
gentle way, that the hill
permits lovers to join.

WHAT WE SEE WHEN HE IS PRACTISING THE KARNATIK RAAGAS HE IS LEARNING

Vasanta

He sings,
notes sprout,
they leaf and
flower;
they fruit,
they ripen;
in her eyes,
in her ears,
in her hidden
chest,
birds, cows,
bees, wasps,
crows, ants,
worms, the
roots of
growing
things
all stretch
towards
light and sap:
Vasanta.

Todi

He sings;
wind swirls
and snarls,
lightning snags,
thunder pushes
rain to strike arrow-sharp
on His chest, shoulders,
the trishulam in His
hands, as he strides,
shaking
earth, sky and all; my
heart stretches, snaps
its chains, breaks its
holding cage and
soars to perch on
His shoulder,
where She,
Daughter of the
Mountains,
hangs lifeless;
sometimes it flies
to his waist, where
his udukkai jostles,
hits his weary bones
and re-sounds:
Todi.

Andolika

He sings;
the notes
fall into line;
they bend and
lift—with brocade
curtains
and tiny bell
tassels all round—
a palanquin of
gold and silver
and glowing
beads and
inside, She—
giver of
speech, giver
of wisdom,
the one
they call Durga.
From above
heavenly flowers
and at her feet,
music:
Andolika.

Malayamarutam

He sings;
she hears birds
calling, leaves
rustling, tree
branches swaying,
the faint smell of
devadaru and sandal;
it seems she can
see mountainsides
thick with forests
and inside the forest,
bees, forest jasmine,
green tulasi and blue lotus,
all embracing their lover,
this wind that comes
from those hills:
Malayamarutam.

Kalyani

He sings;
they look at her
and break into
smiles: her eyes
are twin lamps,
her mouth is a bird
reciting
auspicious names,
her chest is a safe
house.
        In her eyes,
on her wrists, her
nose, around her
neck, on her toes
and in the knotted
curlings of her hair,
the notes shine:
Kalyani.

Bhairavi

He sings;
seated among
all those many
who are
lost in his
song, the
poet looks
around for
Her:
the one
who is boat-like—
the ferry across
life—She
who rides
a lion,
roars like
thunder,
and sunders
all bonds with
one
sidelong glance:
Bhairavi.

Jyotisvaroopini

He sings;
they're absorbed
in the notes,
the turn of phrase,
the fall of beats,
all things she
doesn't understand,
but she knows to
look around,
for what he is singing
sounds like
tonight, She will
come there too—
She whose eyes
are the ferry
that oars us
through life—
and
riding on Her lion,
Her lotus-red hands
will stretch to take
what is Hers:
Jyotisvaroopini.

WHAT THE POET WROTE WHEN THE MUSICIAN ASKED FOR A POEM WITH THE KARNATIK NAME FOR RAAG BHOOPALI, 'MOHANAM'

Were his eyes closed?
Did you feel when they opened, he
would look for you?
Did your eyes close too?
And did he come to you then,
did he tug you by the arm and
lead you, unresisting, down to the river?
Was it dusk when he held you by the
shoulders and turned his heaving lips
towards you?
Did you raise yourself on your toes and
stretch your neck so he could rest
his face in its curve?
Did his hands reach for you, draw back
then, helpless, pull you against the
rampart of ribs guarding his heart's
fortress? Did their hardy doors swing
open as if the touch of your breasts was
their secret key?

Did he whisper things
that made you deaf to everything else,
making you forget
you were trying to understand the quirks
of the scale for Mohana raagam?
Did he pull you down the
stone steps into the water's deep
and embrace you there, pressing himself
into you? And did the fish gather
around to watch this sport?
Did he then, again and again, dip
and lift you—his waist girdled by your legs—
and call your name as delight
rose in his throat, and did it make you—with a
strength you can't always summon—
flip him over and raft him in the water,
swift, so swift he did not know how far down
the river you had taken him
(your legs, your hands parting
the water's flow)
till he opened his eyes and
saw there, far in the distance, the town's
lights, retreating.

Then did he put you onto his back and
swim you to the bank, there to
lift your chin with one hand and look
into your eyes, the other prest into
the fold of flesh at your waist. Did your
heart's fort not try to defend itself even
once? Did you know you would never
be the same again—not the chin he had
held in his delicate hand, nor the curve of

your neck into which he had breathed your
name, not your back, on which his nails
may have left trails, or your feet, which
seem to belong to him, not you?
Was he humming under his breath?

Did you know that unseen by you both, the
afternoon undertow pulled away from its
own surface, or that there was another on the
water's bank, keeping beat with his bamboo
reed, his eyes, the undertow of the world's
current? His name and this raaga
have the same root: moh.

II

Terrain Mapping

WILDWOODS: WHAT HE SAYS TO HER ABOUT LOVE

Prest
to my man's chest
of bones and hardy flesh;
listen, can you hear,
in the mountain
passes of my ribs,
caravans laden with breath,
stopping to read the map
of your embrace?
Can you feel
the creature in my heart
surge to the one in yours,
to plunge—as if by a singled will—
headlong into the wildwood of us?

BAROMETRIC PRESSURE: WHAT HE SAYS HE WOULD LIKE TO DO

In the moment we are permeant with each other, osmotic (inseparable), I want my arms to break free—resolute—to lift you and tumble onto this bed, where we have been solute and solvent, over and over.

As the moult of attire slips floorward and I am entering into you, I want you to stay me, your hands authoritative on my pliant heart, your eyes looking past this—me, this room, us, our union, all—at the now-revealed hint of your in-progress verse that you must grasp, before it goes back how it came.

Then, lying beside you, I want to hear the poem's foundries start up—wood catching in its seasoned fireplaces, furnaces sparking, their vigorous thrums resonant in both your ears. As the scorch of it spreads, and stubborn smoke chokes the wind out of my chest, I want to feel (again) the so-familiar lusty wheeze of my air-sacs, gasping for the air of my song.

GREEN COVER: WHERE HE WISHES THEY COULD BE RIGHT THEN

I want to walk with you in forests full of forest sounds, and
linger near flowers with colours that cities don't authorise.

I want to pass near beehives heavy on high branches, and
feel my fingers start their familiar beat all along your spine.

I want to lean on an old divdhor—to you, *devadaru*—and as
I draw you to my chest, I want you to ask me to sing to you.

TOPOLOGICAL ENTROPY: WHAT SHE SAYS WHEN HE WONDERS AT HOW THEIR LOVE GROWS

Like how
owls, squirrels,
snakes, ants, the stretching
champa,
the spreading jasmine, the
stubborn cactus,
the running stream,
leaves, buds, fruits,
farmers, poets,
women in labour, tailors,
surgeons, horses,
fruit-sellers, halva-makers,
the man in love, the
songster, the geographer,
the barrister's wife, the
mathematician's husband,
the drunk, the consumptive,
the priest, the elephant-catcher
—fie on him—
the night watchman,
the milkman, all grow
closer to death
every moment, moment after
moment after

without doing anything.

UPLAND RELIEF: WHAT HE SAYS HER LANGUAGE SOUNDS LIKE, IN HIGH PLACES

The first time we stood there, on
that crest, looking
out onto the distant purple
of the mountains, my hands were
searching blindly for your waist.
I could have looked down, but at that
moment, it seemed crude to turn my
eyes away from the crimson horizon.
And I stood there—around us, birds,
humans, and in the sky,
a helicopter—thinking you would know
my shyness and arch your hip into my
grasp, but you didn't.
And then, ribbons of mist drifting up
from the valley, you
held my arm, and pulling yourself
up, put your lips to my ear and spoke
in your southern language
and my hands, startled, leaped
to your waist, clasping it to me.

FLORA: ANTARA ON A CURD-RICE AFTERNOON

Some days ago, garnishing,
like you showed me,
curd rice, my fingers, dipping to
the onions in their basket,
began to tingle and leaped right out.
Finding nothing, I dipped again and
again, such a tingle.
Then, shining a torch into basket-dark,
what do I see but an onion, purple
as always,
but from its tip, a green ribbon sprouting.

And standing there, the green in my eyes,
I recalled how you said it felt like
my voice fell into your heart's soil,
and sprouted
into the first poem you wrote about me,
in which you call me to come and watch
the rain, my head in your waiting lap.

Come to me, come see how it grows,
its green tendrils curling, that onion in its
yellow pot, on the front balcony,
where the sun comes first every morning,

come and watch sun-warm
working with green
to make onions the same as all onions,
except these sting and make my eyes
run even before they are grown.

ROUTE MARKER: WHAT HE SAYS ABOUT THINKING OF HER WHEN HE IS AT HOME

Sometimes, when the moon shines,
full and ivory-lit,
my eyes fill and run,
remembering the night on the beach,
in Tutukudi, the white moon, filled to
round, when you told me about
those two lovers, washed out to sea
and washed back three days later,
lifeless, their arms still around each other,
and how you wept on my chest,
my tears dropping silently on your head.

When the wind blows, when the cat
calls from next door,
when the flower-lady comes,
when the milk boils over,
when I look at myself in the mirror,
it seems as if you are here,
your head tilted in that way,
waiting for me to break into song,
and then, I'm searching for the songs I
think will cloud in your ears and break
into flurries of poems.

LANDMARK: WHAT HE SAID WHEN SHE ASKED WHAT HE WAS THINKING OF

In bed with a cold,
last week,
I remembered the night
in that Spanish Airbnb,
when we both woke up
because the sea—so many
floors below us—was so loud,
and you said
if you could, you would
choose to die in the sea;
I said, don't say
inauspicious things,
and then, you bit my lip
and said,
what inauspicious!

SCALE: WHAT HE SAYS WHEN SHE ASKS HIM IF HIS MOOD CHANGES TO THINK OF HER

I was tuning the fifth verse
of the Saundaryalahari—which should
have been no more
difficult than the other four—and
something in that moment made
me think:
these verses would be kinder to
a Karnatik musician.

I don't know why I did that,
and I can't say why it made me feel
so bad. I sat there,
tanpura put aside, my back against
the wall. The black hard-bind was on
the chair, the printouts on the floor,
next to me.
And then I recalled that time in
Vasisht, when we left well before
dawn to trek to the waterfall
and how when we got there, the sun
—just rising beyond the line
of trees—suddenly broke into a
thousand rainbows in the water,
and the old man, our guide, took

something from his pouch
and dropped it into the water
and when we asked, he showed us:
grains of rice, mustard, cloves of
garlic and bits of dry flowers.
Then, he pointed to the
water and to us and said: 'There, also.'

LAND CLASSIFICATION: WHAT HE SAYS ON ANOTHER ANNIVERSARY

Today is August 24, the day that alchemised what
fates we had named *ours*, into mild unfamiliarity
like neighbours' dogs, not ours, but known to us,
and we, to them: our steps, our scent, the treats we
give, or don't give; who we too love, but habitually
from behind boundary walls.

From the other side of this window-frame, the lens
of my eyes measure degrees of sun, sunlight, bird-
dash. My ears spin, threaded by bird call. Were you
here, you'd have got light-headed in the way you do
—and if I reached over and touched you, you would
fold into my curves, press your ear to my chest and
say, paadagan. (Never gaayak)

This sunlight's canister unrolls, as from supply reels,
frames of us: at first; then later. I see you arriving at
our first assignation—at Sharath and Nimmi's when
they and the kids were off on a rare long weekend.
That day I was humming—of all things—the chautal
'Poojan chali Mahadev.' Over the music, it seemed
a voice-over ran on: 'The poet reaches the musician's
friend's house.' 'The poet says she'd been imagining
the first thing they would say to each other.'

Then, you were there, I held the door open, and said to you—of all things—'Andar aayiye', and you peering in, under your breath, muttered, 'Chai nashta keejiye'.

On that day, too—establishing an unaltered template —you set your ear to my chest and said *paadagan*, its syllables streaming, as if towards rivers, seas, onward to oceans of meaning, unlike *gaayak*, which is a dam, its embankments impounding the reserved waters of *hamari rashtra bhasha*.

LANDMARK: WHAT HE SAID WHEN HE WAS STAYING WITH HER, AND SHE BARELY ATE, BEFORE RUSHING TO CLASS

That's all, only that much?
Aren't you teaching Mira's poetry today?
You can't do that on an empty stomach—
her poetry is a hungry beast that goes straight
to the belly, looking for food.
But you know that—for you love like she,
all the world turning into the beloved.
And by that I don't mean to suggest I am like
the god—no, I am Mira too, the entire world
wearing my loved one's shape and voice.

Come, sit here, let me feed you a little
more of this dosa-chutney; open your
kiss-marked lips, eat.

Last night, as you lay with your head
on my chest and your lips spoke against
my ear, my name was a bird that
hatched out of your ribsnest.
You have so many poems
about me, my song and you and
your poetry, and what they do to each
other.

I've no poems, but I know this:
your lips, your ears, all of you, ring and
resound with this language in which,
you explain to me, there are nuances of
differences between the kinds of lover a
man can be:
'iniyan', 'kathalan', 'anban' and 'kannalan'.

Come,
eat just a little more, so that when you're
reading Mira, and she reaches
into your belly, she won't retreat hungry.

LAND CAPABILITY: WHAT HE SAYS WHEN SHE ASKS HIM WHAT HE WANTS TO DO

I want to sit in that room in the hills,
evening purpling outside, with mist,
the sun, faint underneath, and say
to you
something that will make you shut
your eyes, scrunch your face and say:
I wish I'd said that.

CONTOUR LINES: WHAT HE SAID WHEN SHE ASKED HIM IF HE THOUGHT OF THE FIRST TIME THEY MET

I remembered your perfume, after the
Fes Concert,
You should have been here: Kabir Helminsky
came up to be introduced; he was so taken up
with 'Deewana kiye Shyam,'
I offered to Airdrop him the song.

He invited me to dinner. When I told him I had
a friend who admires his Rumi translations,
he said, Why isn't she here?
I asked him how he decided it was 'she',
and he smiled and said, *My friend, I've been*
in the business of love most of my life,
I know.
I'm glad I recognised him before we
were introduced.

When we were sitting out in the garden after
dinner, he said, *So tell me about this friend*
of yours who knows Rumi.
I told him about your new work.
When I was leaving, he said, here, this is
for her and handed me a vial of attar.
Amber, he said and asked, *Do you know what*

amber symbolises?
When I said no, he refused to tell me.
Ask her, he said, *ask her when she's*
in your arms.

I recalled the first time I smelt your
vetiver perfume.
I was walking towards the greenroom
with the others and would have passed
you in a few seconds, but someone
stopped us with a song request;
I was three steps from you,
my eyes drawn to your back, the indigo
of your blouse, your hair, something about
the way you were sitting.
When the vetiver
wafted into my nostrils—I knew it was
yours, though I did not know you yet—
and almost as if to confirm,
you raised your hand just then and
rubbed the back of your neck, and I saw
the surgery scar at your nape, its criss-cross
of stitches that my fingers almost
reached out to touch.

Little did I know then
that you would say to me, not much after,
that I had been
awaited; that in 'the sweetest language of
the South' you had prayed to topple into
future's begging bowl,
for the beggar hungering for you.

III

Border Gods

TRIKUTA: HOW WELL THEY KNOW EACH OTHER

Remember the time they first travelled together
to the town by the sea?
It was raining when she arrived; and he could be
there to pick her up because this was so far south,
it was unlikely he would be recognised.
She came out of the arrival gates and spotted him
immediately—the indigo of his shirt, a flag, herald
of victories beyond the pale, beyond any heralding.

He was looking at her, his lips curved into that
smile he has for when things go the way he wants
them to, and then his eyes, hovering over her face,
began to gleam and she knew his first kiss that
morning would go to her pink mukkuti—his gift to
her on his birthday.

YOGAMAYA: SHE STAKES HER CLAIM

I should be seated there,
on your right thigh,
my left arm snaking over your left
shoulder, my left breast, the one
with the birthmark, pressed to
your ribs; I should drop my head
a little towards your shoulder
like She and She and She do when
they are seated on the godly thighs
of their spouses. I should be limpid
to your murk, I should be feed for
the songbirds in your chest, I
should be cling in your sinews: I
too should be es-spoused.
Seat me on your sinewy thigh,
snake your hand along my back
and rest your fingers on my right
breast, the one without
the birthmark. Spouse me to you.

MANMATHA: THE WAY HER MIND WAS CHURNED AND THE BUTTER OF LOVE DRAWN OUT

The musician sang of Her—the Mother of All—
in His divine chest, homed—He, the trident
bearer,
bull-vehicled, and She, trident bearing too,
her vehicle the gentle lion, sun-ray maned.
And his voice, when it sang of them,
covered its head in a beaded headdress and
cast its eyes down. It seemed to her then that
she was his, and all other women, others'.

When he sang of love, ecstatic, and his
voice—which spun, swirled, soared high and
dipped low, led by the lyric hand-in-hand—
leaped on a
waiting steed and galloped into the poet's
heart, it seemed to her then, that she was
his and all other women, others'.

When he sings, mountains loom, clouds
drift, oceans ebb 'n turn, and sun, stars and
moon come and go, as decreed.
His song does to her what light and green
sap do inside plants: it skips through the
foodways and the waterways of her heart,
and it seems to her then, that he is hers,
and all other men, others'.

KATTABOMMAN: WHAT SHE MAY HAVE BEEN HINTING AT

When you sing,
I am on horseback, soon to be mid-field
of raging battle,
sword swinging, armour gripping
my drumming heart.
The air is ringing with cries of 'Viravel, Vetrivel!'

The Lord of Panchalamkuruchi,
my king, has just some moments ago, ordered,
'Pomurasu olikkattum,' then
the battle drums sound, and we're racing
to battle foes who may fall under our onslaught
or we, under theirs.
His commander-in-chief, I ride the kingdom's
swiftest horse and carry the surest swords,
one in hand, one belted to my
seasoned waist.

I am fearless when I ride into battle—the king
behind me.
Bounden to put my life ahead of his, I allow
myself neither fear nor doubt;

bounden to put my honour where he does,
I allow myself no mirror but his will.
When he calls aloud, 'Por! Por! War! War!'
I ride out ahead, sword in a brandish above
my head.

I do not turn back to see who stands there
behind me, waving, perhaps weeping.
I have wound bands across my chest
to keep my woman's breasts from weeping
for the man I leave behind now, and forever
if I do not re-turn from battle.
Perhaps my king, behind me, turns back
and waves, perhaps he makes a sign of
reassurance to the man I love. That I will return.

MATHAVI: HE KNEW WHAT SHE WAS ACTUALLY SAYING

When you sing 'Najaria laage nahin kahin aur,'
someone who can,
banishes me into unmapped territories
between the lines, after handing me a
bagful of words to barter passage back home.

My words dive into the Vaigai and come up
beside the toe-ringed feet of she who will
burn a city. She asks:
Can you write the sorrow of losing a partner?
When you sing,
something rips up my maps, and breaks
my compass and takes me out of my way.

So, when others are gathered to view the
spectacle of the hero's wife about to raze a very
ancient city
—beloved of poets—I am at another place,
giving ear to his 'other' woman speak.
She says: *I will burn no cities.*
She loved—knowing he was hers;
I loved him, knowing I was his.

The fire will barter her a place in this city's
memory.
My place was in his heart and now: no more of me.

When you sing, in the nowhere between the lines,
I find myself in the company of people
who appear to have been expecting me:
all of them expendable
beyond the making of an artwork,
but this your-voiced 'Najaria laage nahin' tells me
this is the home of poets and their
characters, all of them, both in and out of place.

ROOPMATI-BAZ BAHADUR: THEY BOTH KNOW IT'S ABOUT POETRY AND SONG ALSO

When you sing Bhimpalasi,
hawks swoop from high
crags down to my side,
ignoring
my writing wrist, which I
make offer.
And are those
sparrows I hear, through
the sirening of spring's first
kuyil?

When you sing Bhimpalasi,
how do I become all the
women and men who have
lost colour,
pining for their lovers?
And how, a little while
later, do I become
spring-hued couples, their
eyes telling tales of joining?

When you sing Bhimpalasi,
I can hear in the distance
Baz Bahadur sing to
Roopmati,
both turned towards the
land she gave up for him.

When you sing Bhimpalasi,
the irresistible Ravana
reaches into the basket of
his belly and
prises out his guts, to
music his god's forgiveness.

When you sing Bhimpalasi,
in my head, many
voices go: write, write, write.

BAGESHRI: WHAT SHE WROTE WHEN HE WAS GOING BACK HOME, AND SHE TOO

When you sing 'Sakhi man lage na', in Bageshri,
on the top of the high mountain to which she
has retired, she sheds her anger
and then she can look down into the valleys and
call his name;
she can tell her companions—the tiger, the deer,
the mountain crow that comes to drop fruit into
her lap, the geese that slow overhead
like a salute—
how she loves him so; that even the mountains,
the stars, the high mountain birds, the honey in
familiar flowers, the moon's glow that warms
her to the bones, how they all wither under the
burn of his absence.

When you sing, her voice makes the clouds feel they
too are crying for him, they stop and lean down,
they gather her words and carry them pressed close
to their airy bosoms—to him
as he stands looking out over his land, his people,
and when they pause overhead, there will
be rain in his mighty chest, and in the orchards and
fields of his ribs, her voice
will fall and sink, to mix with its waiting mud, again.

NILA: WHAT SHE SAID WHEN HE ASKED HER IF ANY OF THIS MADE SENSE TO HER

This is my favourite class;
the same class to whom I showed the first poem
I wrote to you; they said, 'It seems very personal
and intimate, thank you for showing it to us.'
They do not know that when I stand here, to teach
them, how tough it is to not say:
Become bowls of beg, well-spiked arrows, be whatever
it takes to claim love.
If you come to this class, you might find me a little
scattered,
because when you said to me, 'Be mine,' I seem to
have forgotten what I was barring out, and barring
in.
In this class that I taught bhakti to, saying how every
god is to be disregarded, until the time he says,
'I long for your work; leave it with me,
let it take up a place in my days,' little do they know
how at times I am almost on the brink of telling you:
'I want only you, I'll even let my words take up with
someone else.'
Only on the brink though, always.

This is my class and I, their teacher, and here I am,
uprooted heart, mud, and all.
In this language I teach in, I cannot say to them:
'Lean such that you topple into future's begging bowl,
to await the beggar who hungers for you.'
But I've said it to myself in the sweetest language
of my South, and here you are.

KUBERA: WHAT SHE WROTE, WHEN THE MUSICIAN ASKED HER TO WRITE HIM 'A VERY CHEESY POEM'

When you sing,
I am won over by
time's quiet pleadings:
from the side of
the marauding poet
hordes (riding in and
pillaging)
I come over to the side
of the gentle host, who
waits on the Beloved.

KUBERA: AND ANOTHER ONE, BECAUSE THE FIRST WAS SO SWEET

When you sing, I become no one.
If you looked for me, they would turn
and say, 'Oh, she was just here, and then
we don't know what happened.'
When you sing, all things stay where
they should, doing what they ought,
but the thing that keeps *then* from
now, and *now* from *later*, comes
undone and I'm between endless
births and in each one you're singing.
When you sing and I'm floating—
neither now, nor then—between worlds,
awaiting births, no one knows how, but
each time, I'm allowed to be a poet.
If you ask for me, they'll turn their faces
to you, look into your eyes and say,
'She was here and then she wasn't.'

KUBERA: AND A THIRD ONE, BECAUSE THE FIRST TWO MADE THEM HAPPY

How well he is versed
in music,
the whole world knows;
but how well she verses
he alone knows,
because
for him alone,
she verses whole worlds.

KUBERA: AND A FOURTH, BECAUSE SHE WAS FEELING AMUSED BY HER OWN ABILITY TO BE UN-SELF-CONSCIOUS

Somewhere where she stopped
they told her he had passed that
way and left something for her,
when they brought it to her
wrapped in a roll of cloth
she knew before it was unwrapt
that it would be the book she
had once asked him for,
the one in which he wrote
his dreams and in which he
described how he had been seduced
time and again by the
notes of raagas that seemed to lie
in wait for him.
When she held the book to her
chest, she could feel them
swoop and land on her shoulders, sharp claws
drawn in: sa, re, ga, ma, pa, dha, ni,
soon they would say his name in her ears.

YAMA: WHAT THE MUSICIAN SAYS WHEN HIS FRIENDS ASK HIM ABOUT HER, THE POET, AND HIS MUSIC

Old words come back into my vocabulary,
like little and big creatures returning to drink
at familiar waterholes, through the alterings
of the seasons.
I hum lines from songs in my language—not
part of my concert stock—as if I'm thinking
ahead to a time when she asks to hear what
my grandmother and aunts, my mother, sang.

In the terrain of what we do, our languages run,
sometimes down the ravines of our limitations—
crashing, torrenting; sometimes in torpor as
we are enclosed in the lure of us, sometimes
it seems we are a library
of speaking dictionaries, and words dislocate
from their pages to float overhead, raining down
a somewhat-benediction.

There is a song I remember my mother singing,
'Love's madness is air; indeed, air is love's madness.'

NIRRITI: WHAT SHE WROTE WHEN HE ASKED HER IF SHE EVER THOUGHT OF BEING WITHOUT HIM

When you don't sing,
there is a line at the door of the Sufi,
who is stopping briefly in town,
and I am at its tail end.
What if he leaves before my turn comes?

I am not myself:
what shall I do with this empty room
where my heart used to live?
what shall I do with my breath that can't
seem to make the climb up my throat?

You'd think I was made entirely of bones
—the way I rattle.
My head spins so fast, I fear it may spin
off its bony handle.
My hands and legs don't seem to know
they belong to me;

I dream of strange things and start
from sleep, and so often
I don't know where the parts of me
I cannot recall, went.

They told me, when the Sufi looks, he knows;
they said he always has in his bag,
just the cure for your ailment.

When you sing, he sees me loitering,
and somehow makes me turn my head
and look at him:
he seems to be looking right inside my
emptied nest of ribs and it seems that bird
who used to live there is winging
back to its home.

He takes my trembling hands
and clasps me to his soft chest; he says,
'My dear poet, here is the horse your teacher
left for you, and here, the birth chart your father
left, and this is the waistband with the love charms
that your mother gave into
my care.
And here is the only thing you should take now—
this scroll that the man with desert winds in his voice
left for you:
an invitation to hear him sing on the night of the full moon,
at the palace of the dervishes.'

When you sing, one by one swirling dervishes step onto the
floor
of my drumming heart, and I recall where I last sat and wrote
the poem about the Sufi arriving in town with instructions to
wait till the ailing poet went to him for an antidote to
lovesickness.

INDRA: WHAT SHE WROTE, AFTER THEY HAD READ THE MEANINGS OF MANY SWATHI THIRUNAL PADAMS

Dear Swathi Thirunal, it could be like this too, you know:
Oh, moon-faced girl, whose lips utter words so sweet,
the bees just can't stay away,
go to him—the one who had my heart—tell him how
I have been waiting for him.
Tell him that I beg him to remember his promises; do
not hold back anything, my
dear girl. Tell him—in that clever way you have—all that
he needs to know now.

Go tell him this: the large cupboard in my bedroom is
full of his clothes—the dandy,
he insisted on storing a full wardrobe here in the days
he was visiting me.
Do tell him to send someone and have it removed. He
will, I know, fuss at length
if I give it all away, else I could have done that and saved
us the trouble. Sigh.

Inform him I need that space for the collection that's
come to me from Grandfather.

I want that cupboard as the early morning sun has a
way of lingering there
which is good for the palm leaves. Tell him that I could
have it all packed to go
but I have seen him fuss over the folds of his robes so
much, it's better not to.

Tell him to return the gifts I gave him: he will never have
use of them, never has:
the Telugu rendering of the Tathagata's nature-sermon,
gifted by Bhatti Anjaiah;
Draksharama Shastrigaru's Telugu-Sanskrit-Tamil lexicon,
done for Grandfather.
He has to return the sixty-four padams I authored for him.

Ask him to give it all back, the man has not read a word in
his life, he gets neither poetry
nor philosophy, he would do anything to not deal with it;
but his knowledge of perfumes,
jewellery, weaves, of flowers and the varied honey they
produce, of music and dance and of the
pleasure-spots in a woman's body: this has no parallel.

But you see, for women like me, with minds so like bees,
nectar does not dwell
only in the lotus-eyed glances of good-looking men, or in
the fire of their bodies,
but also in the flowers of their intellect. So, tell him, dear
girl of seasoned speech,
which strikes like a well-aimed dart, to turn from the mirror
and pay heed to this:
return my books and take his clothes, ornaments, perfumes.

IV

Disputed Territories

BADLANDS

It is springtime in the orchards: you can
smell the worms stirring in their mud;
with a buzz, sunwarm settles on tree-backs
and wall-laps.
The lake must be brimming, lotuses and all.
The poet's scrolls are at her side, awaiting her
stylus; the musician's song is in his belly,
awaiting voice.

Of course, the poet and the musician are like
lyric and tune—like what ink must be to paper.
They're as if made for each, the other only.

But have they—musician and poet—or we,
who witness all this, ever thought:
what of her, the first one, the other one?
What if it is she who is the binding for the
pages of his life, that without,
he may come undone
and be carried off in an untuned wind?

MARSHES, BOGS, SWAMPS

She fears they will come to visit her;
ring her doorbell and smile—though she's
said she's busy, and she won't be able to
summon a smile in return, because maybe
she will be making love to him, and will
not be able to unlock her legs from his
involved waist.
Or maybe he's lowering her onto the mat
and she will be engrossed in his dhoti's
white, falling, and his eyes, still dressed
in the song he just finished.
Or maybe he's entering into her, and
settling, and she is deaf to everything but
the march of his breath, from the caves of
his lungs, through the mountain mouth of
his throat, to her lips.
She fears they will come to her door smiling
and speak to her in their language, which
is hers as well, the oldest of the southern
tongues—in which he must stay on the outside.

DENSE VEGETATION

Now, you've reached inside and got my guts in
your fingers like Ravana, except that lovely one
had his own, not his lover's.

Now you've shut your eyes, closed me in those
song-lined vats to stifle, ferment, bubble and
wait, like Sita in the garden.

What we don't realise, none of us, is that you,
Ravana the mighty, and Sita the balanced, all
are archetypes, my love.

What am I that I am gutted, caged and sent to
brew in garden vats? Surely archetypes are
their own ferment!

Now, you've opened your eyes and let me flow
into the waiting cup of your lips, there to stir
with breath and bubble.

Don't shut them, the doors into the archetypal
garden where all are us: the rejected lover, the
affronted loved one, the musician, the poet, and
the hapless reader.

INACCESSIBLE TERRAIN: QUESTIONS FOR HER

Why, when he sings, do you feel you're in the path of that song, being knocked out of yourself? Why, when he's asleep and you're not, do you sometimes feel that he's a warning you should heed? When you look into his eyes, jewelled with bright tears, as he grasps the wayward notes—nostrils flared, hands clenched—why does it sometimes seem to you like the shout-out of a very quaint romance, whose hexed heroine clambers out of her proper bed to follow the golden-throated hero, into exile from home?

Why do you remember tales of lovelorn heroines who hesitate to look in their lovers' eyes, for fear of seeing there, images of other women, why do you remember stories of how they wait—faces averted, while the men dip and rinse their eyes in rivers that never stand still?
Why do you never recall these lines that ended an earlier poem: 'I am a poet, and for me, everything is a poem in waiting. I want to look into your eyes—where other women may still be lingering, as if at the doorways of greenrooms, from which you will exit—and see them all leave, foot-by-ankleted foot, disintegrating under the seismic shuddering of my language.'

Could it be that you fear that while love has added to itself a vitality, which collects and flows as moisten does in the stemways of plants that store for seasonal aridities, it may have torn the potent join—the caudex—of your words, spilling words, word-glue, word-sequences?

RAVINES: WHAT SHE FEELS, SITTING IN THE CONCERT HALL, LISTENING TO HIM

That she often wants to go up on the stage, take his hand,
steal him away from those clapping rasikas and—God
knows why—also wants to take off the ornaments from her
ears, her neck, her fingers, waist and drop it all to the floor
of the concert hall, all except the pink-stoned nose-stud
he gifted her, his first gift to her.

That she wants to lie in the waves of her favourite beach,
without imagining/wishing she could sit with him in the
snow falling on the slopes of his home;
that she wants to take him to the house where she grew
up and for a while think he might take her to his.

That she wants to sit with him on high hills and tell him
how she has poetried He Who Lives on High Hills, and
in the Heartscave;
that she wants to know what lies waiting, in the darkest
corners of their fears. And so on.

That she is not sure why she can't let go of what stops
her from reading him this line from her notebook: 'I
want to be the girdle of you, like the
oceans that girdle the earth, holding and rocking every tide.'

ESCARPMENTS: WHAT SHE WRITES AFTER HE SINGS JOGESHWARI

When you sing Jogeshwari, and the Jog and Rageshree that make it what it is, begin to diverge, I recall another birth: the one in which I received lessons on writing from my master. You know him, he composed that priceless tale that we here in the South celebrate—the one about the anklets, which led to a king falling dead for letting shringara deafen both of his ears to dharma; and led a woman—who thereafter became a goddess—to burn the city where she had lost her husband to that unheeded dharma.

Jogeshwari makes wife-husband images gather and pool in my mind; it makes me recall my father's dislike of this raaga and its inventor: 'that sitarist who left his godly wife'. It also —of all I remember of that other life—brings back echoes of my master's warnings about poets who believe that their poems will one day become their lives, or the reverse of that.

Jogeshwari, with its apparently husband-wife purva-ang and Uttarang, spreads out a map—not with the brown and orange of forests and mountains, but the blues and yellows of states and borders—and asks me how I hope to arrive at a domestic arrangement with this man—from a north, further than I have gone, and his northern language—singular and mountainous.

Perhaps I fear this question not because it has no answer but because I fear I have more of my father's either-or, this-or-that than I care to admit. But let's leave him out of it, for raag Jogeshwari is not either-or, fusing as it does Jog's urge to be united and Rageshree's to be unentangled, free to soar, to go. I will not lend myself to my father's way, but rather to Master's, for he had the words to write love between one man and two wives, in the tale he made up with what was and what could.

GORGES: WHAT HIS DETAILING OF THE STHAYI OF RAAG DURGA BRINGS TO HER MIND

When you sing Durga,
I'm filling my quiver with sharpened arrows;
I remove my jewelled waistband and pull on armour.
See, here on my chest, the insignia of my clan—
the yellow kondrai.

When you sing Durga,
I am at the border of my kingdom, on my
impatient battle horse. I know that if I die in another's
land, they will send, with honours, my body home, to
the mud of my ancestors.

When you sing Durga,
the fierce Vaigai slows to kiss its green banks
which cry, 'Stay, stay'. I bend into her eddies and make
what offerings I must.

When you sing Durga,
I lean closer to the mirror and adjust, on my waiting
chest, now un-armoured, the jewels my mother and
her mother once wore.

When you sing Durga,
my heart is a battle horse returned home; a locket
ancestral—like its chain of gold—knocks against
my breast, your face within its in-closure,
hidden from all eyes.

When you sing Durga,
I wish I were deaf to its warnings of crocodile-filled
moats, of hefty doors shutting to intruders, the
familial interiors of your language, where
you and she cohabit.

SOFT SEDIMENTARY ROCK: WHAT SHE WRITES WHEN HE ASKS FOR A POEM IN THE MOOD OF THE MADHYA LAY JHAPTAL MALKAUNS BANDISH HE IS SINGING

When you sing Malkauns, I am kneeling,
forehead pressed to the kindly feet of one
I have found after much searching; one
who promises to free me from the shackles
of what we so easily #karma.

'Rise, child,' says my Master, whose hands,
now gesturing benediction over my
shaven head, will soon wrap me in white,
hand me a begging bowl, a wooden staff,
and with that, a new name.

The man I loved stands there, so dry-eyed
it might seem he doesn't love me,
but that would not be true: his eyes are dry
because he is a poet who has wept—broken
heart rattling—in poem after poem.

For the same reason, he doesn't ask, 'How
could you do this?' Or 'Don't you love me?'
Maybe he too uses #karma to make sense
of it all; maybe being a poet, he does not

require sense to be made.
Like all of us, he waits for what we've
been told will save me from doing what I
have done life after life:
my new name.
I do not want to be a Jyotirmayi, Dayamayi,
Santimayi, Anandamayi, or a Maitri.

It's time now: my master's hands raise me,
she bends her head to kiss my forehead.
At the touch of her lips I recall, as if yesterday,
my mother kissing me just there when
I uttered my very first word.

It seems as if yesterday, too, that he who
stole me away from my mother and stored
me in his vast arms, kissed me, not there,
but on my silent lips, and shutting both of
his eyes, said: 'Say my name.'

My master turns me towards the crowd
to make the announcement; her grip on mine
tightens when I turn to look at he, the poet,
once mine. To me, then to the crowd, she
calls my new name: Shunya.

They say many waiting poets wrote of this
event of my being named out of life. Maybe
they made sense with #karma. Perhaps
somebody in the crowd played a bandish
for the occasion, with raag Malkauns.

SHIFTING RIVERS: WHAT SHE WROTE WHEN HE ASKED FOR A POEM, WITH SITA IN IT, AFTER HE'D SUNG THE MANJH KHAMAJ 16-MATRA TULSI BHAJAN

There, across the waters, in an island kingdom ruled
by a musician, whose wife is a scholar even the gods
envy,
under a tree on which are flowers and loud birds,
she sits.
Around her are other women—who read, sing, paint,
wrestle, riddle, string buds, string instruments, run
after deer, dogs, children, and voices they recognise.

On this side of the waters is the one who strung his
bow and won her.
When the sky's light turns red, he will call halt to all
parleys, then wash, and ankle-deep, in the swirling
waves, he will offer routine thanks to his many gods.

Under the Ashoka, she writes, stylus following the go
of her thoughts. Soon they will come to see her, the
scholar-queen and her husband—king and musician.

They will call her neither 'Rama's wife' nor 'Janaka's
daughter', but 'Sita, dear Sita'. She wonders what they
will say when she tells them of what she's writing: a
poem about a hunter fated to transform into a poet.

SHIFTING RIVERS II: WHAT THE POET WROTE WHEN THE MUSICIAN ASKED FOR THE POEM SITA IS WRITING

In an old forest
—there will I set the scene of the transformation.
Let the hunter be made to see that he has nothing;
then let him go till the paths stop.
Untongued by sorrow, there let him sit. Let the forest
wrap him in mud, let him beg the trees to teach him to
speak again, let them teach him how to call out to them:
maraaa maraaa
maraaa maraaa maraaa maraaa.
And as he speaks, let him see when he finishes one
maraaa, another sprouts—its roots grabbing a hold on
his tongue, spreading in its caudexed veins.
Let him know that it is not *maraaama raamaraama*
conveniently breaking into *maraama raamaraama*, but
maraaa: with trunk and spreading branches,
into which birds will in, to nest
like the words fated to him, nest in a future forest.
When he repeats, hearing its sound, its roots stirring
his tongue, *maraaa maraaa maraaa maraaa*, then,
he will see that the forest is all: God and word, fate,
everything.

HIGH ALTITUDE GLACIATED TERRAIN: WHAT THE POET WROTE AFTER HE FINISHED SINGING FOR HER, A DRUT LAY KATHAK KAVIT

Without palanquin or accompanying trumpets,
but
draped in brocade and wrapped in silk, the bride
leaves home and goes—on roads not used to royal
traffic—to the house of the man who has just won
her in a tournament of bows and arrows.
She's at the door of a poor man's house—five men
at her side—she, already having
selected the one with whom to share her mind.

When you sing—one woman worth more than a
kingdom and kings—accompanied by five men,
who will give her up for a kingship, a kingdom, a
crown, together they wait for a mother, who will
say—before opening the door to them—as if to
total strangers: 'Sons, share these spoils equally.'

When you sing, he—the hero—on one of the many
moon-lit balconies of his palace, stands looking
out over the kingdom, once his friend's, now his.
When you sing, I see him there, he whose mother
opens that door and instructs his five brothers to
share by five, the prize got by one among them.

After the last note has stilled, I am surprised that I am dry-eyed, though in my head there is a wail of words that seem to be warning me that I am at a threshold, where there is neither a welcome nor opening doors, nor speech that invites me to be one among those who live inside.

V

Monumentation

TERMS OF REFERENCE

What is it that entrances one, the other?
Is it the music & lyric, or is it he himself?
Is it the words & sense, or is it she herself?
Or as the seekers ask: is it actually their
very particular nature, their specific fates?

How is it that when he rushes headlong,
in his throat, song's shamanic goad, she
is an entranced oracle tracking her speak?
What, when he bleeds, makes her feel cut?
Is it that they are two bodies, one soul?
Or as the seekers say, when two have seen,
together and similarly, what language
means & does, then they become joined,
like stalks at their caudex, in-closing a
seasonal store of wet now, for a future arid.

TERMS OF REFERENCE II

Love in noun get-up is a flying chariot; it is a magic
helper and untold treasures;
turned out in verb costume, it is last-minute tickets,
clandestine airport pick-ups and destinations where
he will not be recognised.

Love journeys from noun's hibernations into verb's
up-and-abouting, and then curls back again into the
nounsleeve, and again.

Love's impel forces an untying of the knots that keep
their living tethered, when they ought to be grazing;
it brings home what of their life they send outdoors to
pasture, when they ought to stay and still.

Does love work in their work? Does it swell song and
poem? Does it do to them, as they do to it: does it pay
heed, pay tithes; will it pay—if need be—with its life?

PRIORITISATION OF ACTIONS

When he is singing, and she sits—as she's wont to—watching the
blue sky turn round and dark with rain,
she must remember that when its shell cracks to let rain pour,
she should not make associations to *break*:
what might break her, him, their relationship's shell, such kinds
of break.
She should learn to let her eyes fall on these creepers, spring
buds ready to flower, without wondering:
Have the yambarzal blossomed in his homeland, has she walked
beside their waving yellow—she, his sanctioned half, joined,
blessed and in-stated by families and world.

When he is done singing and comes to lie with his head in her
lap, he will hear what her guts're saying.
She should be told to get into English mode, be stiff upper-lipped,
to stop her heart, turned round and black, from pouring all over
its foreign decorum.

When they are done with kissing and other intimacies, he must
return and she too must turn back, to the lead lines of songs and
of poems, for without those, we fear that the seasons of their love
will not remember to turn, to change stanza and beat.

BOUNDARY STATUS

He should, of course, use English when he's speaking
of his love,
for in his language, and in hers—when love is being
spoken of—time, angels, even God, will speak along.

They should also know there are things he will need
his language for:
For example, in English, how will he say to her and
have its sense mean just as it does in his language
—that when the birds of her speech soar into the vast
orchards of his chest, it does not feel 'spring-touched'
and not at all 'spring-visited', or 'spring-blest' or even
'spring-hued' but rather, 'spring-ridden'.

How will a reader not stumble if he said, in English,
that when he sips from the vessel of her eyes, he
knows that their tears taste different if his lips are
singing?

In due course, they will want to say that he knows he
has become hers, and she, his.
At that point, do tell them to say it twice, in both of
their tongues, for language is the sickle that can cut,
basket, thrash and store the grains of them.

For other things and times, for other occasions, let
them return to English, which all things considered,
has come to them with good references:
it has been trained to stay, to serve, to clear up, and
to create semblances of order in the house's hold.

BILATERAL CO-OPERATION

Do not look at her when you sing 'Deewana kiye Shyam'—
latch the cage of your eyes, lest they fly off to her face,
their raucous wings drawing rasikas' heads to them,
and to her.
When you sing 'Babul mora naihar chuto hi jay', and
you toss and catch the syllables of 'naihar', their
air-borne curves varying with every repetition, and
your musicians smile at the masterful jugglery of
the bol-bant, you will both remember your home—
the many leave-takings it has stood stoic against
(though your people could stay).
She will remember her friend, most of whose family
were hard-pressed to take leave, to find other homes
to re-settle, move down to the ocean-girdled South.
Your eyes are accustomed to stop the tears that strain
to run, but hers are not.
Do what you must: pick another bol to explore, to
display the charms of artistry; try not to look at her.
Do something,
do it quickly, and mind you, no half-measures: art is not
enough to make up for the reçognition that though it can
move hearts and minds, and even perhaps alter flesh
and blood—making the implacable helix tremble—it can
do nothing to alter
the chapters of history, or the lines of our jagged geography.

RESOURCE ALLOCATION

When he draws out the notes of a Bhairavi, or a Behag
or Kalavati and sweat forms on his brow, she wants to
rub her forehead to his and have their liquid fates mix,
to blend with him, bewitching note by drawn-out note.

When a Darbari or a Malkauns or a Yaman engulf him,
she wants to be the tendrils of silence that he clutches
to keep from drowning;
she wants to be flowering vines twining over his hands,
legs, his chest, his still-sweating face and singing lips.

This is our recommendation: when he draws out these
notes of familiar raagas, and sweat breaks on their brow,
it is imperative that she tells him: you have to be mine.

REITERATION OF OBJECTIVES

Let him sit at her feet, lean back against her legs, put his
head in her lap; let her wipe the sweat off his forehead,
on which she is fated now.
Let her fingers circle his eyes and latch up all the gates he
unlatched to let love run wild—bolt from its many-gated
corral.

Let her lips move over the slopes of his cheeks on which
a thousand eyes put up tents when he sings, to sweep up
all traces of camping.
Let her embrace his body with hers, so that the creatures
in their bones may travel from one to the other ancient
province: of song and poetry.
Let silence bind them in its clasp; when he draws her down
to him, let them be sealed into a contract of breath and flesh.

PRINCIPAL RECOMMENDATIONS: FOR HIM

Don't let the hounds circling her heart—their
abandon—distract you.
Ask to be announced, instruct your language
to herald you, win you a ritual welcome,
a place at the hearth;
a favoured seat for you and your God, who
is Singular and bracing, like mountain air.

After many crossings of thresholds—of place,
of time and language—wrapt and cossetted in
acquired grammars of loving,
lay yourselves down, and what passes between
her lips and your song-ribbed ones,
gather and sow into the tracts of your days.

In time, you will both be moved to tell your
love—'Naan unnai kaathalikkiren,' she will say,
in that old southerly tongue, which we now
learn is more ancient than we were told,
to which you will reply with words that have
resounded in the booen-lined gardens
and walkways of your far-northern home:
'Me chhi chaene maay.'

What remains will be to ensure a flow of sap
in the xylems and phloems of this love—to
go on—carrying blessings of continued crop
to you both, for you both.
For you both, ameen, and ameen and ameen.

PRINCIPAL RECOMMENDATIONS: FOR HER

Know that under your human tangle of locks and cranial bone,
an oracle of love is seated, her fang-mouthed head tilted to
catch your asks.
Lure her out into the bright of day, edge up close and lift your
face near—mouth ajar in the hope of a benediction.
If you're lucky, she will strike—her bite sharp, deep—and you will
stagger from the venom speeding into the many stems and
caudexes of your tongue: the ritual vessel for her reluctant boons.

When the oracular-ed tongue speaks you upstream, towards those
headwaters, where the runnel of language pools—there, your legs
will buckle, and you will find that you are kneeling as you strain
to speak your ask, and you will be surprised by how long it takes
for the rill of your own love-spelled words to stir.
When you turn back downstream, you will have understood that
you must set aside the truth of love, and turn to the half-truths and
the fictions of loving, for that will do for your love poem what green
sap does for growing plants.
You will have acquired the daring to pick up the gauntlet that love—
with a mocking turn of wrist—flung before you.
You will approach the love poem—alone, well-armed—for combat by
idiom and artifice; you will meet every cutting word strike for strike,
and give your all to the fight, because you need what this victory
promises: a definite separation of dominions between love and
love poem.

FOOTNOTE

When he sings to her in his language,
and she in her language recites lines
that have companied her writing,
it seems as if both sets of ancestors leave
their graves in the mud of their family
homes,
and come to sit beside them:
knowing listeners.
It seems that from the two ends of this
land that is home to them both,
birds and animals arrive, circle overhead,
or trample over the useless crop-leavings
of the past.
Then, like the shoals of fish that follow
their radars into hospitable oceans
are gathered into its watery embrace,
language clasps them to its roiling chest.

POSTSCRIPT

Before settling into *Boundary Commissions* with its five sections—'Data Collections', 'Terrain Mapping', 'Border Gods', 'Disputed Territories' and 'Monumentation'—this collection changed titles, sectioning, and language many more times than any other work of mine.

When I started writing this note, I recalled an earlier, now-abandoned poem titled 'How to Write a Love Poem', hinting at an existing pre-occupation with the logic of the love poem, which I attempted to explore in a series of questions about the role of experience and memory and their somewhat shifty/shifting partnership in the writing.

Should you love yourself first, turn and say to you: Your spell binds, stays?
Should you recall that old love, its canker still resistant to the cauter of other men?
Should you make your way to the dungeon where you've kept her chained,
the you that loved him still, when he wasn't to be loved anymore?

The sum of this and later trialling made two things clear, without which these poems would not have been as they are: the necessity for me to mark the distinction between speaking love and speaking of love, and to insert the reader into the text's, and by implication, love's momentums. The lovers in the poems cannot address each other, even when they are, but must address the reader always, for the reader is the recipient of the language of the love poem.

For me, the logic of writing—as of life—is always that of language, and the reasoning for all the reworking I did came from musings about language. I enjoy the process of editing, starting with the editor's feedback and then working, labouring over the changes. I do not show my work while I am writing and even afterwards, and the first person to read it is always the editor. And while I enjoy such praise as may be given to the writing, it is the comments about what may not be working that excite me. Somehow, that entrance of another person into the writing is necessary at the point when I am done with the draft, to not become distanced from it, for the recluse in me is also reclusive to writing and language. After months of co-habitation with it, I am frantic to retreat into some literal and imaginative seclusion, where I do not want human language. The tension of the editorial invasion—for want of a better word at this point—is both a call to arms and a seductive offer of worldly charms. I may perhaps be at my writing best in that period of bookwork.

The editing of this collection was affected by my brother Jayan's suddenly dying: I couldn't allow too much simplicity in the poems; there had to be spots of inexplicability, as of fate, the same one that took my sibling.

This note would not be complete without my acknowledging the camaraderie shared with my sharp yet indulgent editor Karthika, who it seems acknowledges that I may sometimes be spaced-out and casual during the writing and manuscripting, but will be rigorous in the reworking, by never rushing me, and by offering suggestions that intrigue. I was undecided about the ordering of the sections, and it was Karthika who moved 'Data Collection' to its attractive position at the start.

I also want to express my deep appreciation for the ease and efficiency of being represented by Mita Kapur, of Siyahi, with whom this is my first book.

As always, language it seems is my primary ideal, god, inspiration, friend, companion, and whatnot. As I grow closer to it, I understand that its mystical hospitability spreads into the mundane, and I have felt it in the work of these poems.